KILLER ANIMALS
PIRANHAS
ON THE HUNT

by Lori Polydoros

Reading Consultant:
Barbara J. Fox
Reading Specialist
North Carolina State University

Content Consultant:
Deborah Nuzzolo
Education Manager
SeaWorld, San Diego

Capstone
press®

Mankato, Minnesota

Blazers is published by Capstone Press,
151 Good Counsel Drive, P.O. Box 669, Mankato, Minnesota 56002.
www.capstonepress.com

Books published by Capstone Press are manufactured with paper
containing at least 10 percent post-consumer waste.

Library of Congress Cataloging-in-Publication Data
Polydoros, Lori, 1968–
     Piranhas : on the hunt / by Lori Polydoros.
     p. cm. — (Blazers. Killer animals)
     Includes bibliographical references and index.
     Summary: "Describes piranhas, their physical features, how they hunt and kill, and their role
in the ecosystem" — Provided by publisher.
     ISBN 978-1-4296-3392-5 (library binding)
     1. Piranhas — Juvenile literature. I. Title. II. Series.
QL638.C5P57 2010
597'.48 — dc22   2009000951

Editorial Credits
Christine Peterson, editor; Kyle Grenz, set designer; Bobbi J. Wyss, book designer;
     Svetlana Zhurkin, media researcher

Photo Credits
Alamy/Krys Bailey, 22–23
Ardea/M. Watson, 21
Peter Arnold/BIOS/Dominique Delfino, 13; Biosphoto/Yan Hubert, 14
Photolibrary/age fotostock/Morales Morales, 6, 16–17; Flirt Collection/John Madere, 10–11;
     Oxford Scientific/Rodger Jackman, 25
Photoshot/Bruce Coleman/Tom Ulrich, 28–29; Wolfgang Bayer, 18–19
Shutterstock/Bonita R. Cheshier, cover; Dmitrijs Mihejevs, 8–9; Tina Rencelj, 26–27
Visuals Unlimited/Kjell Sandved, 5

TABLE OF CONTENTS

ON THE ATTACK!

KILLER FACT

Piranhas often hunt in large
groups of up to 100 fish.

A **school** of piranhas swims in the Amazon River of South America. A few herons sit in a tree high above the water. One of the birds plunges into the murky water.

school – a large number of fish, feeding or moving together

With a burst of speed, hundreds of
piranhas attack. They take quick bites out
of the bird with their razor-sharp teeth.
They scrape away feathers and meat as
they **devour** the heron.

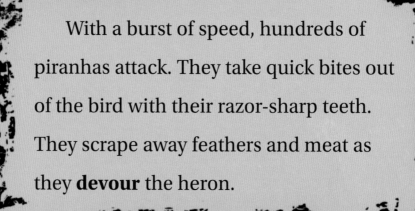

KILLER FACT

The red-bellied piranha is the most
aggressive piranha.

devour – to eat something quickly

A KILLER DESIGN

Piranhas are fierce hunters. Most piranhas grow up to 2 feet (.6 meter) long. They weigh about 7 pounds (3 kilograms).

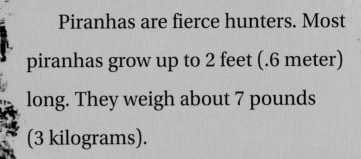

KILLER FACT

About 20 kinds of piranhas live in the Amazon River.

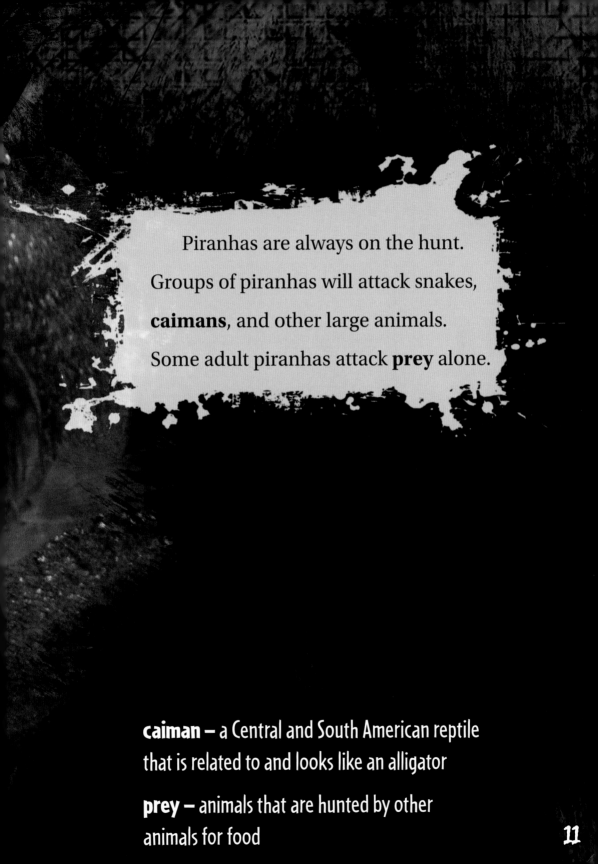

Piranhas are always on the hunt. Groups of piranhas will attack snakes, **caimans**, and other large animals. Some adult piranhas attack **prey** alone.

caiman – a Central and South American reptile that is related to and looks like an alligator

prey – animals that are hunted by other animals for food

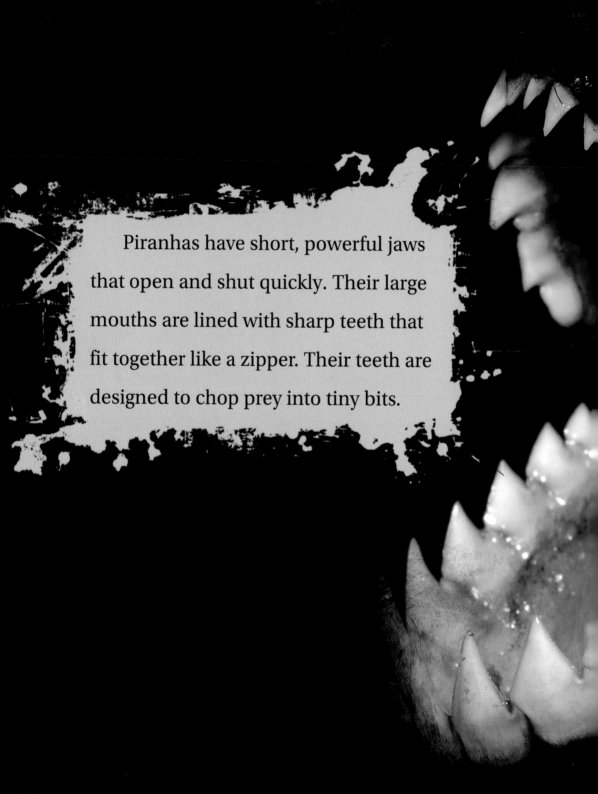

Piranhas have short, powerful jaws that open and shut quickly. Their large mouths are lined with sharp teeth that fit together like a zipper. Their teeth are designed to chop prey into tiny bits.

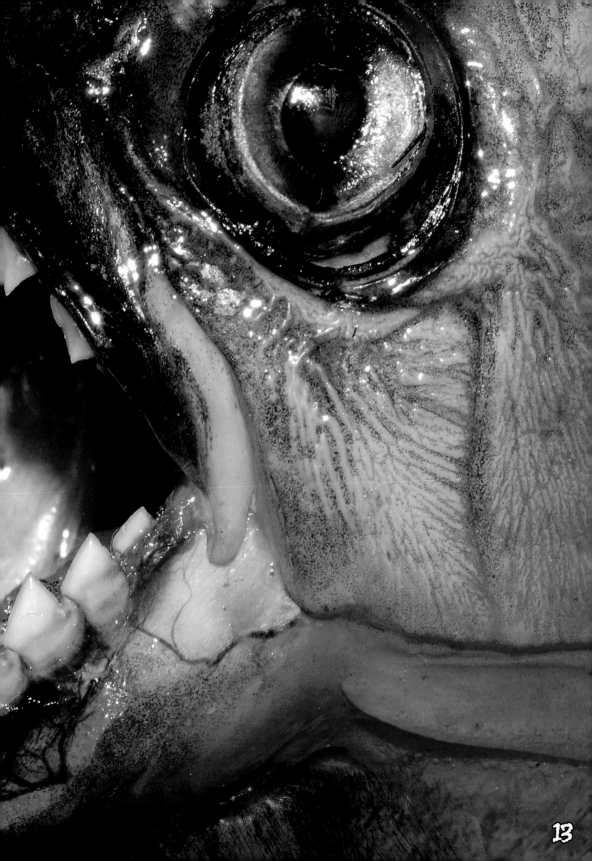

13

Piranhas mainly hunt in the early morning and the evening. They find prey with their senses of smell and hearing. **Sensors** on the sides of their bodies also help them find prey in the muddy water.

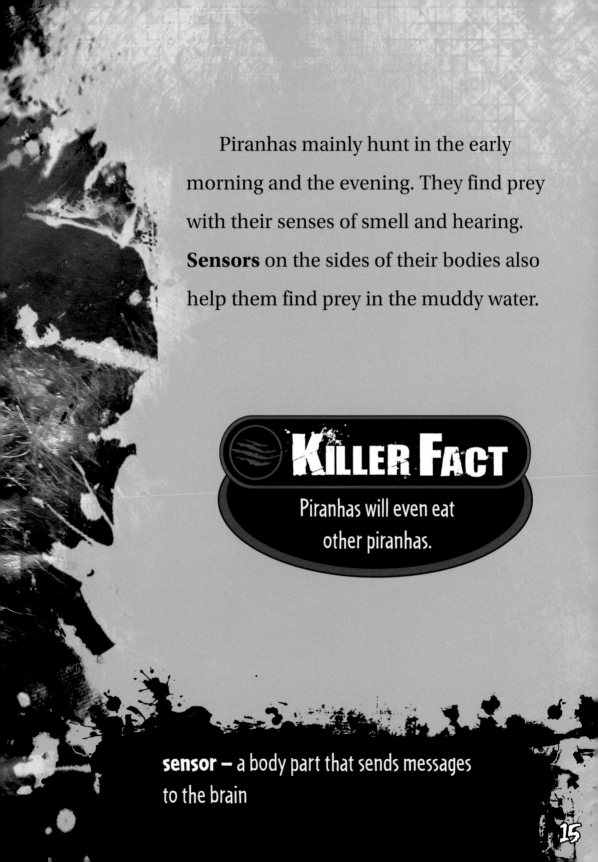

KILLER FACT

Piranhas will even eat other piranhas.

sensor – a body part that sends messages to the brain

Piranhas dart through the water looking for prey. When an animal splashes, piranhas sense the motion. They target the animal. The fish speed through the water to strike.

Piranhas also attack land animals that come to the river to drink. As the animal drinks, piranhas clamp onto its face. They pull young or weak animals into the water and continue their attack.

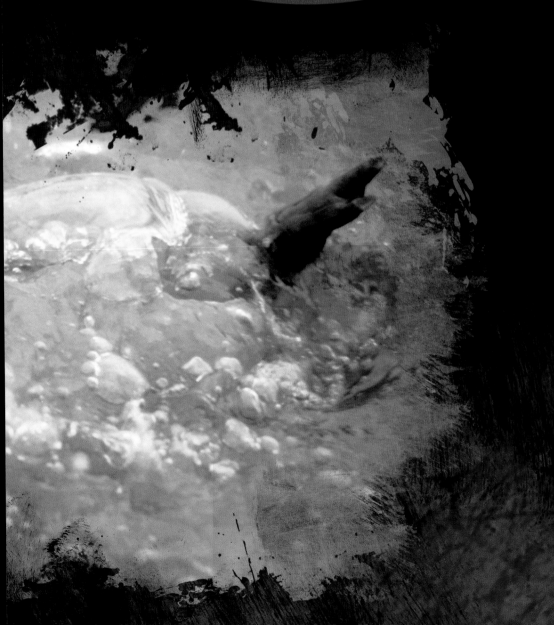

KILLER FACT

Piranhas can chomp off a
human finger in seconds.

Piranhas become more aggressive hunters when prey is hard to find. In a feeding **frenzy**, the hungry fish can strip the meat off an animal in 60 seconds.

KILLER FACT

Piranhas often eat dead animals they find in the water.

frenzy – an often wild or disorderly activity

Piranha Diagram

powerful jaws

dorsal fin

shiny scales

IN THE WILD

Piranhas often eat sick or weak animals. By eating weak animals, piranhas leave more food for strong animals. More food helps stronger animals survive.

KILLER FACT

Piranhas rarely attack people.

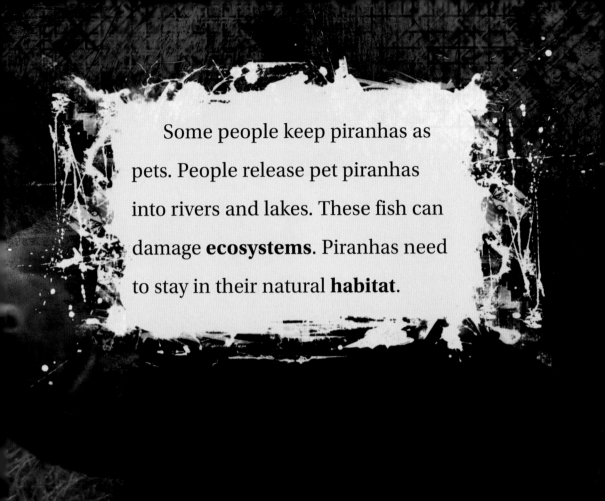

Some people keep piranhas as pets. People release pet piranhas into rivers and lakes. These fish can damage **ecosystems**. Piranhas need to stay in their natural **habitat**.

ecosystem – a group of animals and plants that work together with their surroundings

habitat – the place and natural conditions in which a plant or animal lives

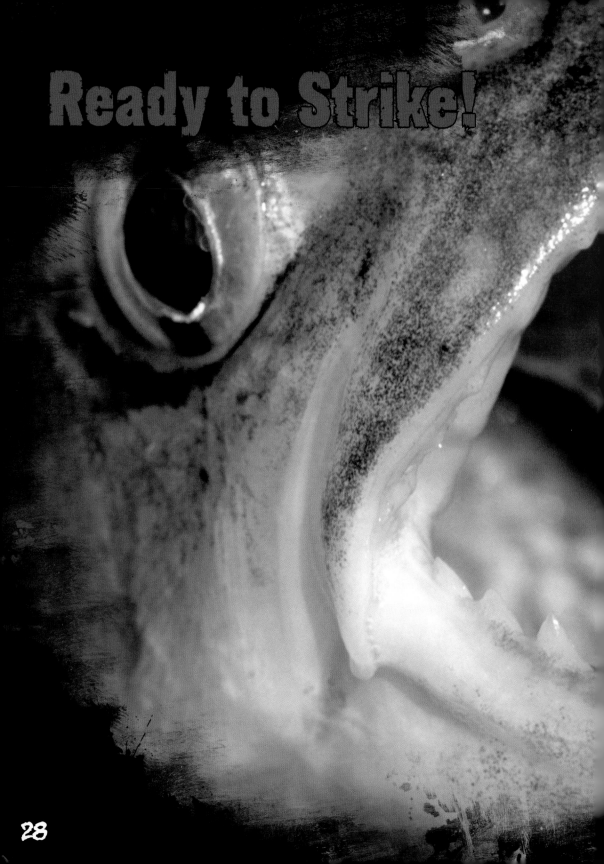

Ready to Strike!

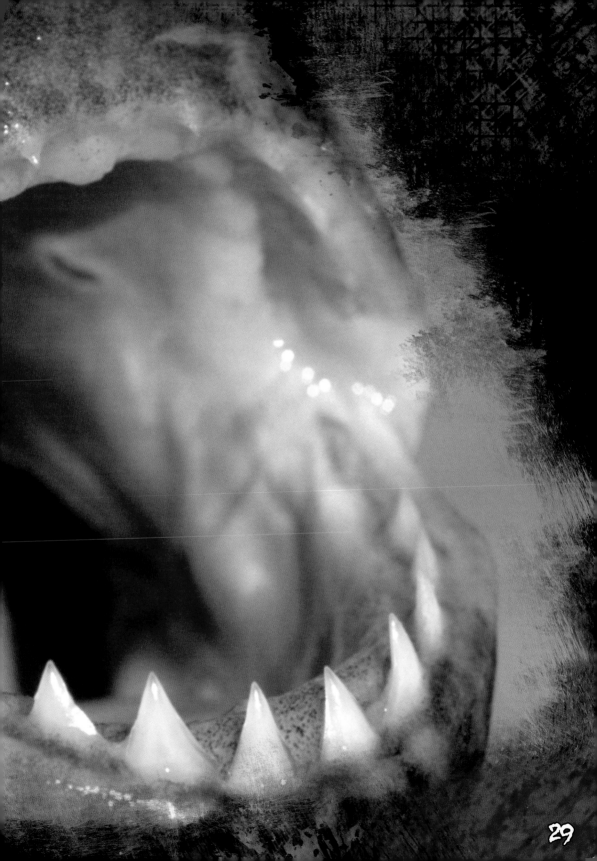

GLOSSARY

caiman (KAY-muhn) — a Central and South American reptile that is related to and looks like an alligator

devour (di-VOUR) — to eat something quickly

ecosystem (EE-koh-sis-tuhm) — a group of animals and plants that work together with their surroundings

frenzy (FREN-zee) — an often wild or disorderly activity

habitat (HAB-uh-tat) — the natural place and conditions in which a plant or animal lives

heron (HER-uhn) — a bird with a long, thin beak and long legs that lives near water

prey (PRAY) — an animal hunted by another animal for food

school (SKOOL) — a large number of the same kind of fish swimming and feeding together

sensor (SEN-sur) — a body part that sends messages to the brain

READ MORE

Berendes, Mary. *Piranhas.* New Naturebooks. Mankato, Minn.: Child's World, 2008.

Chancellor, Deborah. *Piranhas.* Extreme Pets. Mankato, Minn.: Black Rabbit Rooks, 2009.

Schulte, Mary. *The Amazon River.* Rookie Read-About Geography. New York: Children's Press, 2006.

INTERNET SITES

FactHound offers a safe, fun way to find Internet sites related to this book. All of the sites on FactHound have been researched by our staff.

Here's all you do:

Visit *www.facthound.com*

FactHound will fetch the best sites for you!

INDEX